HOODWINKED

STUDY GUIDE

HOODWINKED

Ten Myths Moms Believe &
Why We All Need to Knock It Off

STUDY GUIDE ✑ SIX SESSIONS

KAREN EHMAN & RUTH SCHWENK

ZONDERVAN®

Contents

How to Use This Guide

Group Size

The *Hoodwinked* video study is designed to be experienced in a group setting such as a moms group, Bible study, Sunday school class, or any small group gathering. After viewing each video together, members will participate in a group discussion. Ideally, discussion groups should be no larger than twelve people. Occasionally you will be encouraged to break into smaller clusters of three to six people each for more heart-to-heart sharing and Scripture study. These times are clearly noted in the guide.

Materials Needed

Each participant should have her own study guide, which includes video outline notes, directions for activities, and discussion questions, as well as a reading plan and personal studies to deepen learning between sessions. Participants are also strongly encouraged to have a copy of the *Hoodwinked* book. Reading the book alongside the video curriculum provides even deeper insights that make the journey richer and more meaningful (also, a few of the questions pertain to material covered in the book).

Timing

The time notations—for example (18 minutes)—indicate the *actual* time of video segments and the *suggested* time for each activity or discussion.

For example:

Individual Activity: What Is God Saying to Me? (3 minutes)

Adhering to the suggested times will enable you to complete each session in one hour and fifteen minutes. If you have additional time, you may wish to allow more time for discussion and activities, thereby expanding your group's meeting time to an hour and a half. If you are also having refreshments and a time of sharing prayer requests, figure another thirty minutes.

Facilitation

Each group should appoint a facilitator who is responsible for starting the video and for keeping track of time during discussions and activities. Facilitators may also read questions aloud and monitor discussions, prompting participants to respond and ensuring that everyone has the opportunity to participate.

Between-Sessions Personal Study

Maximize the impact of the curriculum with additional study between group sessions. Carving out about two hours total for personal study between meeting times will enable you to complete both the book and between-session studies by the end of the course. For each session, you may wish to complete the personal study all in one sitting or to spread it out over a few days (for example, working on it a half hour a day on four different days that week). PLEASE NOTE: If you are unable to finish (or even start!) your between-sessions personal study, still attend the group study video session. We are all busy and life happens. You are still wanted and welcome at class even if you don't have your "homework" done.

Scripture Memory

Each study includes a key Scripture verse that highlights the topic of the session theme. If you wish to maximize your learning experience, you may attempt to memorize these verses. In order to assist you with this goal, all six verses are printed in the back of the study guide.

You may photocopy this page on paper or card stock and then cut out the verses. (You really creative and Pinterest-y gals may even want to use card stock and then layer them on top of some decorative paper.) Then keep them in a handy place—perhaps your car, purse, or laptop bag. You can practice memorizing them while waiting in the carpool line or at the doctor's office. Or you may wish to post them at your kitchen sink or on your bathroom mirror where you will see them each day. Laminating them will help to keep them from getting ruined if they get splashed. And, for your convenience, they are sized the same as a business card so you can cut them out and keep them in a business card holder.

It may be helpful to have the group facilitator inquire if any participants are attempting to memorize the key verses. Perhaps those members will want to show up five minutes early (or stay after for a few minutes) to practice reciting them to each other.

Bonus Session

Though there are only six sessions of video teaching, your group may desire to gather for one additional meeting—both to review the session six personal study section as well as to celebrate your time spent together during this curriculum. For your convenience, a seventh bonus session has been provided, featuring discussion questions, activities, and themed recipes should your group decide to serve a meal or refreshments.

SESSION 1

Build Bridges, Not Fences:

When Others Mother Differently

Be completely humble and gentle; be
patient, bearing with one another in love.
Make every effort to keep the unity of
the Spirit through the bond of peace.

⚜ EPHESIANS 4:2–3 ⚜

Video: Build Bridges, Not Fences: When Others Mother Differently (25 minutes)

Play the video teaching segment for session one. As you watch, record any thoughts or concepts that stand out to you in the outline that follows.

Notes

Piece by piece we have crafted in our imagination a stunning mosaic of just what a mom should be—one who does things right and whose kids turn out right. There is one slight problem—a mosaic is not real.

In a quest to be this fictitious woman we somehow begin to believe a lot of myths of motherhood that can leave us hoodwinked, hassled, and even heartbroken.

One myth we believe is this: The way I mother is the right and only way.

Sometimes when we think we are "right," we are actually just being self-righteous. And if you follow the ugly thread of self-righteousness all the way to its gnarly, knotted end, you will find it is rooted in immaturity.

First Corinthians 3:1–9 tells us this about divisions in the body of Christ:

- ❀ Divisions distract.
- ❀ They stunt our growth.
- ❀ The issue isn't who is doing what, but are you acting maturely when you interact with someone who does things differently?

John 13:35 says everyone will know we are Christ's disciples *if* we love one another.

We begin to choose sides. The Corinthians said, "I follow Paul," or "I follow Apollos." Today we say, "I follow famous Dr. So-and-So," or "I follow popular Mommy Blogger So-and-So."

Be very careful with the use of the word *never*. We may be placing our order for a big ol' slice of humble pie when we do.

Seek unity, not uniformity.

Run to God, not to the experts. Use experts as resources, not as lifestyles.

Know your place, but grant others grace.

Build bridges, not fences.

Group Discussion (10 minutes)

Take a few minutes to discuss what you just watched.

1. What part of the video teaching had the most impact on you?

2. As a group, name as many areas as you can where moms have strong opinions about the "right" way to raise kids. Ready? Go!

3. Can you think of an example when you thought you knew the right and only way to mother in a particular area—whether it was before you became a mother or since? Describe the situation.

Cluster Group Activity (10 minutes)

If your group has more than twelve members, consider completing this activity in smaller groups of three to six people each.

Have women in the cluster groups take turns reading aloud Ephesians 4:1–6 in as many Bible translations as you can. (You may view several translations on a tablet or smartphone at biblegateway.com.) Have one person record the various words used that describe how we are to treat each other.

❀ What do you learn from recording these particular words and phrases about how we should behave when we encounter a mom who mothers differently than we do?

❀ Are there any guidelines you can draw out of this passage for how we can behave in the future when rubbing shoulders with someone—especially another believer—who has a very different way of raising kids than we do? Can you think of a specific example that pertains to a real-life, current situation?

Group Discussion (25 minutes)

Gather back together as one large group and answer the following questions.

4. What is one insight you gained from the cluster group activity based on Ephesians 4:1–6?

5. In the video segment, Karen mentioned some observations found in 1 Corinthians 3:1–9 about how we sometimes behave toward others. Have someone read the passage aloud to the group. (Consider reading it in a couple different Bible translations.) Then,

say it in a sentence. In other words, craft a sentence that makes an observation or gives a directive based on this passage, and also cite the verse where you found it. Example: When we argue and quarrel with each other, it proves we are letting our sinful nature control us rather than letting the Holy Spirit control us (verse 3).

6. Karen mentioned that we see from this passage that divisions distract. They can certainly distract us from our missions as moms. How have you seen divisions distract moms, keeping them from focusing on raising their kids as they debate with others about the right — or best — way to parent? Tell the group about it. (But be cautious not to name names!)

7. In the video we were encouraged to "be careful with using the word *never*" in our mothering. Truth time! Do any of you recall a situation — as when Karen declared she'd never, ever use baby formula but then did — when you uttered the phrase "I'll never," but then had to eat those words? What happened?

8. In the teaching segment, we were cautioned against using experts as lifestyle guides — adopting every single thing they say as truth and following all of their advice without even praying about it. How can we be careful to use experts as resources rather than authorities with the final word? If you can, offer an example of a question to ask ourselves before following a piece of advice.

9. *"Know your place, but grant others grace."* What do you think of that statement? What are some ways you can "know the place" God has for you in parenting a particular child at a particular time, but can also extend grace to other mothers who differ in their approach?

10. *"Build bridges, not fences."* When it comes to the mothers you know personally, which do you see more of: bridge building or fence erecting? Take a show of hands in the room for both.

    Can you think of a specific way to build a beautiful bridge with another mother rather than erect an ugly fence? For example: a mom who homeschools could send a handwritten note to a public school mom telling her she will be praying for her kids and their teachers each week during the school year. Or, a public school mom could take her children to a homeschool science fair or sporting event to show support for a homeschool mom.

11. Have someone read aloud Luke 6:27–36. How does this passage apply to bridge building with those who may think differently than we do about raising children? Draw out a few principles from this portion of Scripture about how we are to treat others with whom we don't always see eye to eye.

Individual Activity: What Is God Saying to Me? (3 minutes)

Complete this activity on your own.

Take a mental inventory of your life. Are there any aspects of mothering about which you tend to be even a tad dogmatic now *or* about which you were earlier in your mothering days? Checkmark any areas below:

- ❑ Birth plan (drugs or earth birth, home or hospital, etc.)
- ❑ Type of adoption (foreign or domestic, private agency or foster care system)
- ❑ Nursing versus baby formula
- ❑ Cloth versus disposable diapers
- ❑ Infant sleeping arrangements
- ❑ Feeding of children (store-bought baby food or homemade, organic foods only, specific diet—vegan, paleo, etc.)
- ❑ Schooling options
- ❑ Discipline methods
- ❑ Type of church attended
- ❑ Chores (and payment for chores) for kids, or whether teens should have jobs
- ❑ Kids' clothing choices
- ❑ Teens driving, having curfews, etc.
- ❑ Music, media, and technology allowed for kids
- ❑ Dating, courtship, or other plan for teens and young adults
- ❑ Other: _____

Now, go back and star the one or two areas where you most feel God may be prompting you to know your place but grant others grace.

Closing Prayer (2 minutes)

Have one person close in prayer. Then, get ready to learn more in your between-sessions personal study before meeting for session two!

Between-Sessions Personal Study

Scripture Memory Verse of the Week

Each week of our study will feature an optional Bible verse to ponder and even memorize if you desire. For your convenience, all verses are printed in the back of this study guide. You may photocopy that page on card stock or colored paper. Then, cut out the verses and place them in a prominent place—purse, dashboard, desk, kitchen sink—where you will see them regularly. (You may want to laminate them if posting them at your kitchen or bathroom sink or in the shower stall!) You can also keep them in a business card holder.

Consider pairing with another study group member to help you stay accountable to memorize the six verses. You could come a few minutes early to class—or stay a bit longer—to practice your verses with each other. You might even set an alarm on your cell phone to remind you each day to practice your memory verse.

Here is our verse for this week:

> Be completely humble and gentle; be patient, bearing
> with one another in love. Make every effort to keep the
> unity of the Spirit through the bond of peace.
>
> EPHESIANS 4:2–3

Read and Learn

Read chapters one through three of the *Hoodwinked* book. Use the space below to record any insights you discovered or questions you may want to bring to the next group session.

Study and Reflect

1. In chapter one of *Hoodwinked,* the art form of a mosaic is mentioned. In this inventive method, hundreds of seemingly broken pieces of colored glass, stone, or other materials are purposefully put together on a flat surface, creating a collage of color. While each individual piece isn't anything spectacular on its own, when strategically arranged, they combine to make a simply stunning image.

   We women craft mosaics of motherhood when we pick up pieces of information over the years from those we believe to be stellar moms. What qualities and actions have you deposited in your mind's memory bank of a picture-perfect mom? List a few of them in the chart below, along with the mom (or moms) who exhibited each quality.

QUALITY OR ACTION:	MOTHER(S) WHO EXHIBITED IT:

Now, based on the chart, write a sentence that describes the perfect mosaic of a mom, based on all these women and their qualities and actions. How does seeing this description make you feel?

2. Also in chapter one, Karen writes about the woman described in Proverbs 31:10–31. Read these verses and jot down any qualities or activities that she is praised for doing that inspire you OR that intimidate you:

Inspire me:

Intimidate me:

Many biblical scholars assert that Proverbs 31:10–31 is written in the form of an acrostic poem. The word *acrostic* can be defined as a poem, word puzzle, or other composition in which certain letters in each line form a new word or words. In the case of the Proverbs 31 passage, each line starts with a different letter of the Hebrew alphabet. Some researchers think that this was done in order to easily commit the poem to memory so that it might be recited aloud. In fact, the Jewish tradition is that men recited this acrostic as a way to praise the women in their lives—often a husband to his wife—usually on Friday nights before the weekly Shabbat dinner.

How does this historical background information help you better understand the passage? How does it encourage you to know this Scripture might not actually be recounting all the activities this woman did *in one day's time?*

Are you ready to start making sense of the myths you have believed? As with all lies, there is always an element of truth. So we must be discerning. The devil is tricky. These myths we believe are subtle twistings of the truth. Theologian Charles Spurgeon said it best, "Discernment is not knowing the difference between right and wrong. It is knowing the difference between right and almost right." Some of these myths seem almost right, but they are still dead-center wrong. And they can mess with our mothering in the most awful of ways.

HOODWINKED, PAGE 27

3. In chapter two of *Hoodwinked* (page 32), we encounter the meaning of the Hebrew word for wisdom, *chokmah*—it's skill. Read Proverbs 2:1–5 and then follow the instructions provided:

> My son, if you accept my words
> and store up my commands within you,
>
> turning your ear to wisdom
> and applying your heart to understanding—
>
> indeed, if you call out for insight
> and cry aloud for understanding,

and if you look for it as for silver
and search for it as for hidden treasure,

then you will understand the fear of the LORD
and find the knowledge of God.

PROVERBS 2:1–5

❀ Read the passage again.

❀ Circle any verbs (action words) that tell how we are to pursue wisdom/
acquire skill in our lives.

❀ What is the promise given if we do all of the actions you circled? Underline
this promise.

❀ Finally, go back and place a star in front of the verb/action word you feel
you most need to zero in on as you pursue the skill of wisdom. Then,
write out a sentence prayer to God below about this action word and its
relationship to skillful wisdom.

4. As we parent our children, we often encounter moms who go about their
mothering differently than we do. As a result, we may find ourselves tempted
to be defensive about the way we mother or hypercritical of other mothers'
methods. Look up the following verses and then, in the space provided,
record a few words about how we are to treat others as we interact with them,
even if they think or act differently.

❀ Proverbs 15:1

❀ 1 Corinthians 4:12 – 13a

❀ Ephesians 4:15

❀ Ephesians 4:32

❀ Philippians 2:3

❀ Philippians 4:5

❀ Colossians 3:12

❀ Colossians 4:6

The point is to make sure that the path you are on is the one God has planned for you. Let's stop looking to other women and their choices and look to God instead for direction. Sure, pick other women's brains. Read great books. Observe. Weigh and pray. But make sure that you are going to God and his Word for your mothering marching orders. And then? Go forward with confidence—not condescending cockiness—and serve him and your family as you enjoy your unique journey of motherhood.

HOODWINKED, PAGE 52

5. The book of Titus in the New Testament was written by the apostle Paul to one of his trusted assistants, Titus (go figure!), who was serving as a pastor on the island of Crete. It contains instructions for how members of the church are to live and to treat one another, and also how they are to behave in society.

Read Titus 3:1–8. In the space below, record any advice this Scripture contains about our behavior toward others. Also cite the verse where the advice is found.

BEHAVIOR TOWARD OTHERS:	VERSE WHERE IT IS FOUND:

From this same passage, list the various ways God treated us along with the verse where it's mentioned.

HOW GOD TREATED US:	VERSE WHERE IT IS FOUND:

Finally, in the space below, summarize what this passage says about how we are to treat others and why. (Psst. To answer the "why," be sure to note the verses that talk about what God has done for us and how he has treated us.)

One more time for review. Here is our optional memory verse for this week:

> Be completely humble and gentle; be patient, bearing with one another in love. Make every effort to keep the unity of the Spirit through the bond of peace.
>
> EPHESIANS 4:2–3

SESSION 2

Mothering Matters:

Seeing the Hard Years as the Heart Years

....

Let us not become weary in doing
good, for at the proper time we will
reap a harvest if we do not give up.

~ GALATIANS 6:9 ~

....

Checking In (10 minutes)

Welcome to session two of *Hoodwinked*. In order to get the most from this study, please share what you have learned from reading the book and completing your between-sessions personal study. Keep in mind that if you weren't able to finish all of the material, you are still encouraged to attend each session and offer your valuable insights.

- ❀ Are you experiencing any situations that were addressed in the past week's reading of the *Hoodwinked* book? If so, how did you react to the author's perspective?
- ❀ What from the session one video segment most challenged you or encouraged you since the group last met?
- ❀ Did you have any "aha" moments from the questions or activities in the between-sessions personal study?

Video: Mothering Matters: Seeing the Hard Years as the Heart Years (18 minutes)

Play the video teaching segment for session two. As you watch, record any thoughts or concepts that stand out to you in the outline that follows.

Notes

The seemingly mundane and small moments of motherhood matter.

We have a desire to be known.

Exodus 2:2 – 10 tells us the story of Moses' mother letting him go.

- ❀ She knew God was in control.
- ❀ She knew who ultimately had the power of life and death.

Hebrews 11:23–25 reminds us that it was by faith that Moses' parents were not afraid of the king's edict.

- ❀ Moses' mom didn't minimize her role in impacting future generations.
- ❀ Do we see how we can impact future generations?

Psalm 118:8: "It is better to take refuge in the LORD than to trust in humans."

- ❀ Don't trust in your own feelings of insignificance. God gives the final assessment.
- ❀ Live for God's approval!

God's approval matters most.

Don't see these years as *hard* years, but as *heart* years.

God does some of his best work in the hidden years.

Being a mom requires connecting your story to God's story.

Group Discussion (10 minutes)

Take a few minutes to discuss what you just watched.

1. What part of the video teaching really hit home for you?

2. As a mom, when have you felt like gum balls were scattering every which way and you couldn't move fast enough to control them? (Maybe you found your family involved in too many extracurricular activities or you planned an overly ambitious dinner menu while trying to babysit.) Please share your experience.

3. Consider your last week of social media interaction. What was the motive behind most of your posts, comments, or browsing? Do you find yourself ever wanting to make your unseen mommy moments known? If so, explain.

Cluster Group Discussion (5 minutes)

If your group has more than twelve members, consider completing this discussion in smaller groups of three to six people each.

4. How can we cure our need to be noticed? In other words, where do our hearts find satisfaction as we perform tasks that other family members may not see or appreciate?

5. Perhaps none of us has ever faced the exact situation Moses' mother did, but can you share a time you had to trust God and "let go" of your child?

Group Discussion (20 minutes)

Gather back together as one large group and answer the following questions.

6. Have someone read Matthew 6:1–4 to the group. How does this passage apply to motherhood tasks and actions that are unseen by others?

   As a group, use language similar to what is found in this passage but apply it directly to some responsibilities of motherhood. Have members take turns giving sentences. For example: "When I do seemingly endless loads of laundry week after week, I will not announce it with trumpets to my husband or my kids."

7. Listed below are biblical characters who experienced secluded years. Beneath each example, write some notes on how this hidden season might have shaped this person for God's future plan. It's okay to use your prior knowledge of these characters as well as the verses given.

   ❀ Joseph in prison (Genesis 39:20–23)

   ❀ David as a shepherd (1 Samuel 16:11)

❀ Elijah in the wilderness after running from Jezebel (1 Kings 19:4–8)

Now come up with a couple more examples of biblical characters who experienced a season of hiddenness. Record them in the space below.

Do you see yourself in any of these characters? Why? What do you think God is shaping in you during your unseen motherhood moments?

One of the challenges of choosing to embrace motherhood is that so much of what we as moms do goes under the radar or is unnoticed. Nobody is handing out bonuses, writing feature articles, building statues, or even offering a simple "thank you" to most of us.

HOODWINKED, PAGE 60

Individual Activity: What Is God Saying to Me? (3 minutes)

Complete this activity on your own.

What is something said by one of your group members that you know God wanted you to hear today?

List one specific way in your motherhood that you will embrace hiddenness and serve the God who sees.

The importance of what we do for God is not contingent upon how many *people* see what we do.

HOODWINKED, PAGE 60

Closing Prayer (2 minutes)

Have one person close the group in prayer. Then, get ready to learn more in your between-sessions personal study prior to session three!

Between-Sessions Personal Study

Scripture Memory Verse of the Week

Here is this week's verse to meditate on and memorize if desired. (Remember, all the memory verses are printed together at the back of this study guide. You may photocopy them for your convenience.)

> Let us not become weary in doing good, for at the
> proper time we will reap a harvest if we do not give up.
>
> GALATIANS 6:9

Read and Learn

Read chapters four and five of the *Hoodwinked* book. Use the space below to record any insights that stood out to you or questions you may have. You can share these at your next group session.

Study and Reflect

1. In the beginning of chapter four, Ruth describes a time when she was questioned by a bank teller in regard to her occupation as "just a mom." Have you ever experienced a similar question? How did you manage to remember your worth in Christ at that moment?

2. This week's memory verse is Galatians 6:9: "Let us not become weary in doing good, for at the proper time we will reap a harvest if we do not give up." How can the truth of this verse get us through difficult weeks and rough conversations when we might end up feeling devalued as moms, whether we work outside the home or are at home full-time?

3. Read 1 Peter 3:13–17 slowly and carefully, then think about your role as a mother as you answer the following questions.

   ❀ Where should our hearts be set before we even start a conversation with someone?

   ❀ What two actions does verse 15 encourage us to take? How are these two actions related?

❀ What further light does verse 16 shed on *how* we are to do what we are told to do in verse 15?

Now, you might be wondering what *hope* has to do with motherhood. After all, this verse says to "give the reason for the hope that you have." Let's go a little deeper. Look up Hebrews 11:1 and copy it below.

As moms, there sure is a lot that we *hope* for, don't you think? We might hope that telling Bible stories, kissing boo-boos, making meals, and on and on will amount to something. In this hope, we rest on a biblical faith that what we do matters greatly. Though we can't see it now, we can trust that we will "reap a harvest at the proper time." Faith, hope, and "not growing weary" all play a key role in motherhood.

Another way to look at the question, "Are you just a mom?" is to think of that person asking, "What hope do you have in just mothering kids?" If we think of the question in those terms, what might be your answer? Write a brief answer below.

You are now one step closer to being prepared the next time someone asks you what hope you have in the mundane moments of motherhood.

Friends, we have the best "job" in the world, and we must not underestimate the calling on our lives just because what we do often goes unnoticed. God is watching. And *he* notices.

HOODWINKED, PAGE 62

4. In chapter four Ruth discusses a book with the underlying message that raising kids is a nuisance. How do the following verses counteract this thought?

> Children are a heritage from the LORD, offspring a reward from him.
>
> (PSALM 127:3)

> [Jesus] said: "Truly I tell you, unless you change and become like little children, you will never enter the kingdom of heaven."
>
> (MATTHEW 18:3)

> But Jesus called the children to him and said, "Let the little children come to me, and do not hinder them, for the kingdom of God belongs to such as these."
>
> (LUKE 18:16)

How might you apply these Scriptures the next time you are tempted to think that your children are hindering you?

5. In chapter five of the book, Karen says we should not try to be "mommy-er than thou" with each other. Write the first sentence (it's just four words!) of that section in the middle of page 74 (right after point number two). You might want to use all capital letters.

Consider a time that you felt one-upped or somehow in competition with another mom. Read Philippians 2:3–4. Write down at least three ways you could have used this passage to shape your thoughts or actions in that moment.

1)

2)

3)

Remember, the idea of being in competition with other moms does not just apply to moms our own age. It could also be applicable to an older mom, even our own mom or mother-in-law.

Write down one way you're tempted to compare yourself with a more seasoned mom in your life.

Now write down a way you can be humble and, as Philippians 2:3–4 says, look to the other woman's interests instead of just your own.

6. Write a short prayer that honestly confronts the topics of this personal study. Ask the Holy Spirit to prepare you with answers for those wondering why you're "just a mom," to show you the value of motherhood, and to give you the biblical wisdom to never act as if motherhood is a contest.

One more time — here is this week's optional memory verse:

Let us not become weary in doing good, for at the
proper time we will reap a harvest if we do not give up.

GALATIANS 6:9

SESSION 3

At the Top of the Tightrope:

When You Try to Do It All

Be very careful, then, how you live—not
as unwise but as wise, making the most
of every opportunity, because the days
are evil. Therefore do not be foolish, but
understand what the Lord's will is.

EPHESIANS 5:15–17

Checking In (10 minutes)

Welcome to session three of *Hoodwinked*. An important part of this study is sharing what you have learned from reading the book and completing your between-sessions personal study. Remember; don't worry if you didn't get the material all covered. You are still welcome at the study and your input is valuable!

- ❀ What from the session two video segment most challenged or encouraged you since the group last met?
- ❀ What insights did you discover from reading chapters four and five of the *Hoodwinked* book? Share any particular favorites with the group.
- ❀ What did you find interesting or challenging in the between-sessions personal study questions?

Video: At the Top of the Tightrope: When You Try to Do It All (25 minutes)

Play the video segment for session three. As you watch, record any thoughts or concepts that stand out to you in the outline that follows.

Notes

Every mom is a funambulist (pronounced fyoo-nam'-bul-ist). This word is the original term for a tightrope walker.

We moms often believe this myth: I can do it all, all at once.

Ephesians 5:15–17 gives us a grid to run our various opportunities, activities, tasks, and pastimes through.

❀ Be careful.
❀ Be wise.

We become wise by hanging out with wise friends. Proverbs 13:20 (HCSB) tells us, "The one who walks with the wise will become wise."

We become wise by constantly meditating on God's Word, much like scrolling through information on our phones. Psalm 119:97–98 says, "Oh, how I love your law! I meditate on it all day long. Your commands are always with me and make me wiser than my enemies."

We need to be wise in using our time. Our time can often be our enemy. We must learn to outsmart our schedules, controlling our time rather than letting our time control us!

❀ Make it count.
❀ Discover God's will.

Reevaluate as both a mom and as a family.

Do NOT ask yourself, "Am I capable?" Ask yourself instead, "Am I called?" We moms often have the curse of capability!

Around the house, learn to delegate! Often we are moms who do too much because we have children who do too little. Make it your goal to work yourself out of a job. (Karen's goal is that—by the time they are adults—her kids will know how to do the laundry, clean a bathroom, make a casserole, balance a checkbook, and give a speech.)

Live your priorities. Until a century ago, the word *priority* was only singular.

Accept the fact that motherhood has seasons. You can't do it all, all at once.

Funambulists will tell you that the most crucial aspect of walking the tightrope is to locate your center of mass. As women trying to walk the tightrope of motherhood, our center of mass must be Christ.

Like Nik Wallenda, the famous tightrope walker, let's walk the rope constantly praying and also praising God.

Group Discussion (10 minutes)

Take a few minutes to discuss what you just watched.

1. What part of the video teaching had the most impact on you?

2. What various responsibilities, activities, opportunities, tasks, and pastimes do moms try to juggle? Rattle them off out loud "popcorn style."

3. Have someone read Ephesians 5:15–17 to the group. Of the various parts of the grid Karen mentioned from this passage, what one spoke most to you and why?

    ❋ Be careful.
    ❋ Be wise.
    ❋ Make it count.
    ❋ Discover God's will.

4. Can you think of someone who you feel does a prayerful and careful job of walking the tightrope of motherhood without taking on too much at once? Tell the group about this person and what makes the way she lives life as a mom stand out to you.

Cluster Group Discussion (15 minutes)

If your group is comprised of more than twelve members, consider completing this discussion in smaller groups of three to six people each.

5. Take a minute to look over the list below of the various areas where a mom may need to—or choose to—spend her time. Circle the one or two areas where you most struggle with your time or with getting the task done. Cross out any areas that do not apply to you at this time in your life. (Meaning if you aren't currently employed, cross it out. Or if your hubby does the grocery getting or cooking or cleaning, cross it out—you fortunate woman, you!) Space is also provided for you to write out two more areas of your own that are specific to your life right now.

    ❀ Daily time alone with God—reading, studying, or praying
    ❀ Employment either inside or outside the home
    ❀ Housekeeping, including cleaning, laundry, etc.
    ❀ Menu planning, grocery getting, and cooking
    ❀ Caring for kids' needs, whether toddlers or teens
    ❀ Homeschooling or helping with homework
    ❀ Tending to the family finances, including bill paying
    ❀ Work outdoors, including the lawn, garden, etc.
    ❀ Church responsibilities
    ❀ Volunteer duties in the community or in other organizations
    ❀ Caring for aging parents
    ❀ Daily exercise
    ❀ Hobby or pastime
    ❀ Other: _____
    ❀ Other: _____

Go around the group and share answers one by one. For each person, ask these questions: What are you having trouble getting done? Why do you think this is so? Does any group member have any piece of advice for you?

Of all the various duties, activities, and such listed, are there any you think you might need to remove from your plate? Let any members who feel a nudging in this area share their thoughts with the group.

Group Discussion (10 minutes)

Gather back together as one large group and answer the following questions.

6. Take turns having each of the groups give a report on what their group discovered about their use of time. Any of the members may chime in with their findings.

7. Assign different members of the group to read aloud each of the following verses from the book of Proverbs—the Old Testament book that contains many instructions for how to live wisely. After each verse is read, members may give their thoughts on how it applies to trying to balance the various aspects of life as a mom.

   ❀ Proverbs 3:7

❀ Proverbs 4:26

❀ Proverbs 9:9

❀ Proverbs 10:8

❀ Proverbs 12:26

❀ Proverbs 14:1

❀ Proverbs 19:20

❀ Proverbs 22:3

Individual Activity: What Is God Saying to Me? (3 minutes)

Complete this activity on your own.

Ask God to bring to mind any area where you feel you are stretched too thin or a responsibility or activity to which you have said yes and probably should have said no. Write what this is here:

Take a reflective moment to ask God if you need to bow out of this responsibility or stop doing the activity. If you believe the answer is yes, how will you do this? Jot down your plan here. Then, commit to actually following through with it.

Closing Prayer (2 minutes)

Have one person close the session in prayer. Don't forget to follow through on your plan from your individual activity. Then, get ready for your between-sessions personal study prior to session four.

Between-Sessions Personal Study

Scripture Memory Verse of the Week

Here is our optional Bible verse for this week to ponder, study, and even memorize, if desired. (Remember, all the memory verses are printed out for you in the back of the study guide. You may photocopy them for your convenience and carry them with you or post where you will see them each week.)

> Be very careful, then, how you live—not as unwise but as wise, making the most of every opportunity, because the days are evil. Therefore do not be foolish, but understand what the Lord's will is.
>
> EPHESIANS 5:15–17

Read and Learn

Read chapter six of the *Hoodwinked* book. Use the space below to record any insights you discovered, concepts that challenged you, or questions you may want to bring to the next group session.

Study and Reflect

1. In chapter six of *Hoodwinked*, Karen shared the story of a tipping point in her life as a younger mom. She had allowed her plate to become stacked so high

that just agreeing to bake two dozen cookies for an event sent her over the edge emotionally. Have you ever experienced such a tipping point yourself? Briefly describe the incident here.

Looking back, are there steps you could have taken to prevent this avalanche of emotions that resulted from operating at over-capacity level? If so, what could you have done differently?

Can you think of any questions to ask yourself in the future before taking on a new task, responsibility, or activity?

2. Look up and read Ecclesiastes 3:1–9. Why do you think this Scripture gives us a list of opposite emotions and contrasting actions? What main point do you feel the passage is making when it comes to our time?

Next, in keeping with the format of Ecclesiastes 3:1–9, summarize one or two of your many activities, responsibilities, and emotions in a way that is applicable and memorable to you. Example: There is a time to clean the kitchen and a time to let the dishes sit so I can read to my child instead.

Now read Ecclesiastes 3:11. Write it down in the space below, but before you do, decide which one of the words you need to jump out at you in all caps. The NIV version of this verse reads, "He has made everything beautiful in its time." Might you need to capitalize EVERYTHING—since you feel there are some things in your current life that are less-than-beautiful? Does the word HE need to bounce off the page, reminding you that it is God who works our situations and experiences together in a way that brings him glory and that is best for us? Is it crucial for you to remember that God makes things BEAUTIFUL even though right now in your life many situations seem bothersome instead? Transcribe the verse here and capitalize the word you need to cement in your mind today.

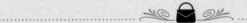

We women are strong. Capable. Clever. Competent. Resourceful. These are all extremely helpful aspects of our selves that assist us in our quest to be good moms. But sometimes these strengths can transform into a weakness because we don't take into account one little thing that we women also have:

Limitations.

HOODWINKED, PAGE 83

3. For each of the following pairs of statements, circle the one that most closely describes your tendencies when it comes to how you spend your time. Although both may be to the extreme, choose the one that most sums up your usual habits.

I usually don't say yes right away when asked to take on a task or responsibility but ponder and pray about it first.	Are you kidding me? The word *yes* rolls off my lips almost as soon as the person asking is through with the question!
Usually, my goal is to create white space in my calendar so I am not over-scheduled.	Most weeks you can't locate white space on my calendar because my days are packed too tightly for even a little wiggle room.
I know my strengths, passions, and likes and try to keep most of my optional activities in line with these.	I fill my optional time with random commitments that I agree to just because they need to be done or so I don't disappoint the person asking.
I am careful to only speak words of correction to someone with whom I have a solid and trusting relationship.	I sometimes correct or instruct people whom I really don't know very well or have a close friendship with.
I feel that how I spend my time accurately reflects what I say my priorities are.	I sometimes — okay often — spend more time on a lower priority in my life and less time with those I feel are important — including God.

4. The book of James was written by a leader in the church at Jerusalem and is full of timeless truths for living a life that pleases God. Read James 4:13–17. What principles can you draw for planning your days from this Scripture? List them here:

Use the directives given in these verses to apply to your current life as a mom. How could you state your own set of guidelines when it comes to talking about what your days hold, or about your plans for the future — or even for the next week?

Verse 15 urges us to say, "If it is the Lord's will, we will live and do this or that." What do you think James means by this?

Is there a danger in using the phrase "if it is God's will" or "Good Lord willing and the creek don't rise" (Karen's mom's favorite saying) when we speak? How can we get to the place where we truly mean what these words convey instead of just tacking them on to the end of our sentences like a magic charm?

5. In this week's video session, Karen offered the following question as a way of helping us determine what place an activity or pastime should have in our lives: "Is this a *tool*, a *toy*, or a *tangent*?" Then she used social media (Facebook, Twitter, etc.) as an example of an activity that could be each one of those things, depending on how you used it. Can you think of an example from your own life of an activity, pastime, or thing that can sometimes be a useful tool, other times serve as an occasional fun toy, but can also morph into a time-wasting tangent? Describe it here.

Look back at what you just wrote. Is there any action step you feel God may be calling you to take about the thing you named? How could you adjust your habits in this area to more effectively use your time or to free up some margin in your too-crowded schedule?

When we learn to hone in on our calling and clear our too-full plate, we can begin to focus on making beautiful music in our life. This includes how we spend our time both inside the home and with outside commitments. We each have a song to strum. We do not need to simply copy the score others around us are following. As we take our concerns prayerfully to the Lord—along with our schedules—he will certainly help us to strike the unique balance that is best for us. He can help us to say "so long" to the striving to be Supermom and help us to discover how to mother in our own distinctive way.

Hoodwinked, page 90

6. In chapter six of *Hoodwinked*, Karen writes:

Not only have I tended to live life too busy, I have also never been a good delegator. I don't know how that came to be; I only know it to be very true. Whether in my home or outside of it, in a committee or work situation, I tend to want to "do it all." Now, it isn't necessarily that I think I know how to do it all, it's more to do with the fact that I want for it all to be done *my* way.

HOODWINKED, PAGE 84

Can you relate to being hesitant to delegate? If so, why do you think you are reluctant to ask for help or to farm out some responsibilities at home?

In the early days of the church recorded for us in the book of Acts, Luke, the author, gives us a glimpse into the growth of the community of believers. We see them taking care of each other, especially the needy. They even share possessions (Acts 2:44–45). But as the congregation grows, so do the number of people who need help. In Acts 6 it reaches a point that the leaders of the church need to determine a solution.

Read Acts 6:1–7 and then complete the following statements by filling in the blanks:

Verse 1: Group number one, the _____,
complained about group number two, the _____,
because group number ones' widows were being overlooked in the daily

_____.

Verse 2: So the Twelve gathered the disciples and declared that it was
not right to neglect _____ in order to

_____.

Verse 3: Their solution was to choose seven men who are described as
_____, and have them take on this task.

Verse 4: This way, the leaders could give their attention to
_____ and _____.

Now, answer these questions, citing the verse where you found each answer:

What did the whole group think of this idea? (verse ____)

What did they then do with the men appointed for the task? (verse ____)

What result did it bring about in the development of the church? (verse ____)

When the family of God hit a logistical snag in caring for its members, they decided to divide and conquer—to delegate. Although the disciples were in charge of the spiritual state of the church *and* its physical operations, they lacked the time to do both properly. Their main responsibility was to lead in the areas of prayer and teaching the Word. However, food needed to be distributed as well. And so, they delegated some duties in order to focus on others. Is there a lesson to be learned here in your own family? If so, what?

Are there any physical operations in your house where you need help in order to focus more time on something else? List a few. For example: I need to assign one of my kids the task of putting away the food and doing the dishes each night so I can use the time to work on my Bible study or deal with the day's paperwork.

7. Our optional memory verse of this week is:

> Be very careful, then, how you live — not as unwise but as wise, making the most of every opportunity, because the days are evil. Therefore do not be foolish, but understand what the Lord's will is.
>
> EPHESIANS 5:15–17

Use the space provided on the next page to craft a prayer based on this passage, asking God to help you to display the characteristics contained in it.

Or, you may want to type your prayer in a notes app on your phone or even make a meme (graphic) of it to use as a screen saver on your computer or as the lock screen on your phone. Whichever method you use, read the prayer regularly over the next several days, inviting God to empower you to use your time wisely and for his glory.

SESSION 4

Pressing the Pause Button:

Taking Your Schedule from Racing to Rest

"Come to me, all you who are weary and
burdened, and I will give you rest. Take
my yoke upon you and learn from me,
for I am gentle and humble in heart, and
you will find rest for your souls. For my
yoke is easy and my burden is light."

≫≪ Matthew 11:28–30 ≫≪

Checking In (10 minutes)

Welcome to session four of *Hoodwinked*. Be encouraged that the group will benefit from hearing your input. Don't hesitate to participate even if you didn't complete all of the reading or study guide questions. We are so glad you are here!

- ❀ What from the session three video segment with Karen were you able to put into practice since we last met?
- ❀ Last week you read chapter six from the *Hoodwinked* book. Share with the group any portion that really stayed with you.
- ❀ What did you find thought-provoking or noteworthy during the between-sessions personal study?

Video: Pressing the Pause Button: Taking Your Schedule from Racing to Rest (17 minutes)

Play the video segment for session four. As you watch, record any thoughts or concepts that stand out to you in the outline that follows.

Notes

Sometimes as moms we feel like a hamster on its wheel.

We may feel stuck and left wishing we could hit the pause button.

Don't miss out on the moments God intends for us to delight in and learn from.

What is rest? Rest is *shalom*, which means peace and wholeness.

Genesis 2:1 – 2 illustrates two aspects of rest:

1. God didn't need rest but rested because everything was as it should be.
2. Time is sacred.

Why should we rest?

Deuteronomy 5:15 helps us understand why we should rest.

1. God brought us out of slavery to observe the Sabbath.
2. Rest brings freedom.

Working hard and being busy doesn't have to mean slavery.

Make time for the moments of life.

How can we rest?

- ❀ Guard our values and our time.
- ❀ Live more proactively rather than reactively.
- ❀ Make a master schedule and write in our values and priorities.

Live on a mission, not in a mess.

Find margins. Live intentionally. Guard actively.

Matthew 11:28–30

1. Jesus is our true source of peace.
2. We won't have an easy life, but we will have an easy soul.

Group Discussion (10 minutes)

Take a few minutes to discuss what you just watched.

1. Was there anything Ruth said that made you think, "Oh yes, that is *so* me!" If so, what was it?

2. Does the definition of the word *shalom*—which means peace and wholeness—give you a new perspective on the concept of rest? If so, in what way?

3. Have someone read Deuteronomy 5:15 one more time aloud to the group. In what area of your schedule are you feeling in bondage? How do you think God could use it as a place to actually bring about freedom?

4. Ruth used this phrase, "Working hard doesn't mean slavery." Do you know someone who is a hard worker but takes time to rest? Are there any qualities that person has that you'd like to integrate into your life?

Cluster Group Discussion (15 minutes)

If your group has more than twelve members, consider completing this discussion in smaller groups of three to six people each.

5. Look back at your notes from the video and answer these questions:

   ❀ What are the two insights from Genesis 2:1–2 that teach us about rest? (Have someone read the verses aloud before you give your answers.)

❀ Keeping these principles in mind, consider the biblical character Jonah. Read Jonah 1:1–6. Jonah was in a deep sleep, but why did God interrupt his slumber?

❀ What might this tell us about the effect disobedience has on our rest?

❀ What might this tell us about rest and completing God's work?

❀ Read Matthew 12:40. How does this connect with the second principle Ruth gave us from Genesis?

❀ Jonah didn't know the significance of being in the fish for three days, but God did. Jesus was pointing us to himself. Every time we take a Sabbath, we enter into that sacred act of pointing toward our Creator. On a scale of one to ten (one = not at all, ten = all the time), how well does your personal schedule point toward Jesus?

❀ What is one action step (big or small) that you are willing to take in regard to balancing work and rest? Share it with the group and ask them to keep you accountable!

Group Discussion (5 minutes)

Gather back together as one large group and answer the following questions.

6. Ask each cluster group to report back on their thoughts of Jonah and his relationship to the topic of rest.

7. Did God reveal anything to you during your cluster group's discussion, perhaps about a time you rested before completing the job he gave you?

Individual Activity: What Is God Saying to Me? (4 minutes)

Complete this activity on your own.

In the video, Ruth used the phrase "live on a mission, not in a mess." Think about your own life. How often do you "live on a mission" in each of the following areas of your life? Place an X at the spot on each continuum that best describes you.

❀ The schedule I keep with my personal quiet time with the Lord

| "I'm in a mess." | "I see some hope." | "I'm intentional most of the time." | "Praise God, I'm living on a mission!" |

❀ The schedule I keep with my husband (if applicable)

| "I'm in a mess." | "I see some hope." | "I'm intentional most of the time." | "Praise God, I'm living on a mission!" |

❀ The schedule I keep with my children

| "I'm in a mess." | "I see some hope." | "I'm intentional most of the time." | "Praise God, I'm living on a mission!" |

❀ The schedule I keep at church

| "I'm in a mess." | "I see some hope." | "I'm intentional most of the time." | "Praise God, I'm living on a mission!" |

❀ The schedule I keep with my extended family

| "I'm in a mess." | "I see some hope." | "I'm intentional most of the time." | "Praise God, I'm living on a mission!" |

❀ The schedule I keep with my friends

●──●
"I'm in a mess."   "I see some hope."   "I'm intentional most   "Praise God, I'm living
                                                      of the time."   on a mission!"

❀ The schedule I keep with my coworkers (if applicable)

●──●
"I'm in a mess."   "I see some hope."   "I'm intentional most   "Praise God, I'm living
                                                      of the time."   on a mission!"

❀ The schedule I keep with my community

●──●
"I'm in a mess."   "I see some hope."   "I'm intentional most   "Praise God, I'm living
                                                      of the time."   on a mission!"

❀ The schedule I keep with social media

●──●
"I'm in a mess."   "I see some hope."   "I'm intentional most   "Praise God, I'm living
                                                      of the time."   on a mission!"

❀ The schedule I keep with _____

●──●
"I'm in a mess."   "I see some hope."   "I'm intentional most   "Praise God, I'm living
                                                      of the time."   on a mission!"

❀ The schedule I keep with _____

●──●
"I'm in a mess."   "I see some hope."   "I'm intentional most   "Praise God, I'm living
                                                      of the time."   on a mission!"

Consider how you can make an improvement in one or more of these areas. Write any thoughts below. Next week, come prepared to discuss your progress!

Closing Prayer (2 minutes)

Have one person close the group in prayer. Be sure to pray about putting action to what everyone has learned. Then pray that everyone has a meaningful and rich time in her between-sessions personal study.

Between-Sessions Personal Study

Scripture Memory Verse of the Week

Here is this week's verse to write upon the tablet of your heart. Since our verse this week is on rest, it might be fitting to keep a written copy of this verse on your nightstand. (Remember, all the memory verses are printed in the back of this study guide. You may photocopy them for your convenience.)

> "Come to me, all you who are weary and burdened, and
> I will give you rest. Take my yoke upon you and learn
> from me, for I am gentle and humble in heart, and you
> will find rest for your souls. For my yoke is easy and my
> burden is light."
>
> MATTHEW 11:28–30

Read and Learn

Read chapters seven and eight of the *Hoodwinked* book. Use the space below to jot down any insights you unearthed, concepts that cut to your heart, or questions that you can carry to the next group session.

I asked the God of the universe to intersect my life with His revelation,
then got up from my prayers and forgot to look. Forgot to seek Him.
Forgot to keep my heart in tune with His voice and His invitation.

(cont.)

All because of the chaotic rush of my day.

When all life feels like an urgent rush from one demand to another, we become forgetful. We forget simple things like where we put our car keys or that one crucial ingredient for dinner when we run into the grocery store. But even more disturbing, we forget God.

LYSA TERKEURST, *THE BEST YES,* PAGE 10

Study and Reflect

1. This week's memory passage (Matthew 11:28–30) is a powerful reminder of where we get our peace. Let's take a look at a man who truly traded shackles for an easy soul. In your Bible, please slowly and carefully read Luke 8:26–39.

    This is a remarkable story. A man who was demon possessed was restored to sanity by Jesus. That is the story in a nutshell, but there are some profound takeaways for us and for how we keep our schedules. Here's the first one:

    When something other than Christ is running your life you will experience alienation.

    Our schedule is what we *do*. If Jesus is not driving what we do, then something else will. Take just a second to reflect on that. Where did the demons often drive this man? (end of verse 27 and end of verse 29)

    He was in desolate places because of what was driving him. Have you ever felt alone or alienated because your schedule had worked you so hard that there just wasn't time for ... well ... *people* anymore? If so, write down how you felt during that time period. Or, perhaps you're experiencing such a situation right now. If so, take a few minutes to write down a couple of action steps you could take that might free up some of your time.

The next takeaway:

When something other than Christ is running your life you lose yourself.

What was the man's response when Jesus asked his name? (verse 30)

This man was defined by what had taken over his life! He couldn't remember his identity. When we let so many activities overtake our existence, someone might ask us our name and we might respond, "Soccerpractice Permissionslip Churchpotluck." The best explanation of how this happens is in Luke 9:24:

> "For whoever would save his life will lose it, but who-
> ever loses his life for my sake will save it." (ESV)

Circle the phrase "for my sake."

Surrendering control of our schedule for the sake of anything but Christ is Not. Worth. It. Let's move to the last major takeaway from the story of the man from the Gerasenes.

When something other than Christ is running your life you will look crazy.

What was the demon-possessed man wearing when he first met Jesus? (verse 27)

When we allow craziness into our schedule, it shows on the outside. When craziness comes, it usually is accompanied by a lack of self-control. Before we know it, we are bogged down with many obligations, many problems, and much crazy.

Where did this man finally find peace? Was there a visible change? (verse 35)

What was this man's purpose after Jesus restored his peace? (verse 39)

Well, demon possession and an out-of-control schedule are two VERY different things. However, the takeaways are very relevant when it comes to how we can live life on purpose. This man from the Gerasenes did not have peace—or purpose—but Jesus changed that. Let's revisit these statements:

* ❀ *When something other than Christ is running your life you will experience alienation.*
* ❀ *When something other than Christ is running your life you lose yourself.*
* ❀ *When something other than Christ is running your life you will look crazy.*

Consider what the Holy Spirit is saying to you through this story. How do you think God would want you to respond? Write your thoughts below.

2. On pages 96–104 of *Hoodwinked*, Ruth gave us a look into her heart by listing her top priorities. Take a little time right now to write out your vision, goal, or purpose in list form, much like Ruth did.

3. To keep from losing sight of our mission, Ruth instructs us to ask ourselves four questions before taking on a new responsibility. Circle the one that jumps out most as one you need to learn to start asking yourself regularly.

    ❀ Does this complement or conflict with my mission?

    ❀ What will this cost my family right now?

    ❀ What will this cost my marriage right now?

    ❀ Am I tempted to say yes for fear of someone's disapproval?

    Why did you choose that particular question?

4. On page 100 of *Hoodwinked* Ruth gives her basic daily schedule. Please create your own basic daily schedule in the chart below, filling in your most important activities for a typical weekday — your nonnegotiables — and the corresponding approximate time slot. Don't include the weekend. An example would be "Bible study and prayer time — 6:30 – 7:00 a.m." or "Get kids up, breakfast, and bus — 7:00 – 7:45 a.m."

NONNEGOTIABLE ACTIVITY	APPROX. TIME SLOT

Now, grab three highlighters or pens of different colors. Highlight or underline all of the activities that have to do with the spiritual growth of yourself or your kids in color number one. Use a second color for those items that have to do with taking care of your family physically. Grab a third color for work done either inside the home to keep it up or outside the home, as employment. What do you learn from your colorful exercise?

5. Read through this week's memory verse—either at the beginning or end of this personal study—and circle all the verbs (action words). Are there more verbs that require action from us or more that require action from Jesus?

In this week's video segment, we were reminded to "guard our values" as well as "live proactively instead of reactively." These things take effort on our part! The very first word of our memory verse is *come*. Just as the man from the Gerasenes came to Jesus, we too must come. As that man found peace, rest, and purpose at the feet of Jesus, so will you.

What does it mean to you to "come to Jesus"?

How will you be proactive in guarding your schedule in the coming week and welcoming the peace of Jesus?

(NOTE: If you would like to go deeper into this subject, please see the Yearly Personal Inventory for Moms at the back of the *Hoodwinked* book.)

Here is a bonus verse for you to meditate on this week. Maybe you want to write it on a sticky note to post in a place you most feel robbed of rest. Is it your bathroom mirror as you get ready for the day? The kitchen where you are busy cooking, serving, and cleaning up over and over again? Or the family vehicle in which you shuttle kids to and fro? Let this verse help to keep your nerves calmed and your mind centered on Christ:

> You will keep in perfect peace all who trust in you, all whose thoughts are fixed on you!
>
> ISAIAH 26:3 NLT

And don't forget this session's memory verse:

> "Come to me, all you who are weary and burdened, and I will give you rest. Take my yoke upon you and learn from me, for I am gentle and humble in heart, and you will find rest for your souls. For my yoke is easy and my burden is light."
>
> MATTHEW 11:28–30

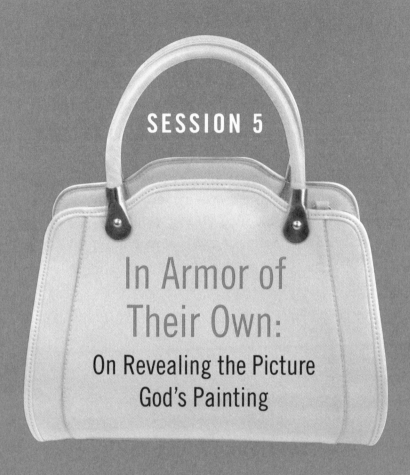

SESSION 5

In Armor of Their Own:

On Revealing the Picture God's Painting

God works in different ways, but it is the same God who does the work in all of us.

୬ 1 CORINTHIANS 12:6 NLT ୬

Checking In (10 minutes)

Welcome to session five of *Hoodwinked*. Be emboldened to share how God is working in your life through this study. As always, please continue contributing to the conversation, even if you weren't able to complete the between-sessions material.

- ❀ What portion of the reading from chapters seven and eight did you particularly enjoy or identify with?
- ❀ In your between-sessions study, you took a closer look at the man from the Gerasenes. Did you find anything eye-opening tucked in that portion of Scripture?
- ❀ Did you make any significant discoveries by writing down your goals and daily schedule? Did it aid you in exposing some important values that you haven't been prioritizing?

....

Video: In Armor of Their Note: On Revealing the Picture God's Painting (15 minutes)

Play the video segment for session five. As you watch, record any thoughts or concepts that stand out to you in the outline that follows.

Notes

As moms we want to control and direct everything, but we must let God work in our children's lives.

Too many times we look at our kids through our own preferences and desires instead of stepping back and letting God do his work through them.

1 Samuel 17:38–39

- ❀ Saul tried to dress David for war, but David wasn't used to the armor.
- ❀ David was resisting the urge to lead like someone else.
- ❀ David had to do what worked for him.

As moms we can act like Saul by dressing our kids in armor they weren't necessarily meant to wear. It takes wisdom, patience, and God's grace to help our children grow into the unique individuals that God made them to be.

Saul's vision for David wasn't the same vision God had. We need to surrender our dream to God's desire. "Not our plan; God's plan."

Remember whose image our kids reflect. We want our kids to reflect God. The goal is to see our kids transformed into the image of Christ.

Connect your child's strengths to God's story.

God used what was already developed in David.

Encourage your kids to use the gifts God has developed in them.

We aren't the original artists. God is. As moms, our goal is to help reveal the picture that is already there.

Group Discussion (15 minutes)

Take a few minutes to discuss what you just watched.

1. What part of Ruth's teaching affected you most?

2. Have you ever had a child build something that took a long time and made a big mess but ultimately made him or her feel more independent? Tell the group about it.

3. Why do you think it is so hard for us as moms to let go and watch our kids create something that is less than perfect?

4. When we do let go and let our kids accomplish something on their own, what immediate benefits emerge—both for us and the child?

5. Have someone read aloud Romans 12:2. Consider the content of this verse and what we just heard Ruth discuss. How do we foster an environment where our kids can be "transformed by the renewing of their mind" and "transformed into the image of Christ"? Give specific ideas.

Cluster Group Discussion (10 minutes)

If your group has more than twelve members, consider completing this discussion in smaller groups of three to six people each.

6. During our last cluster group time we were challenged to take one action step in living by a schedule that pointed toward Jesus—with a balance of work and rest. Did you take that one action step? If so, tell about it. (It's okay to turn back to that section on page 68 of this study guide for review.)

7. Now, back to this session. Have a volunteer read 1 Samuel 16:7. Are there any attributes in your kids that you see as difficult but you know God sees in a different way? How do you think God could use those characteristics as strengths later in life?

8. When we're tempted to become frustrated with our kids (those difficult attributes we were talking about), how can we resist that temptation and actually help them sharpen a skill for Christ?

Group Discussion (10 minutes)

Gather back together as one large group and answer the following questions.

9. Ask each group to share a poignant statement that surfaced during the cluster group time. Feel free to write down anything that speaks to your heart.

10. On a practical, day-to-day basis, how do we keep our focus on what God wants for our children and not what we want?

Does anyone have an example of a time they tried to put their "armor" on their child and it didn't fit? What happened?

11. Think back to the video portion where Ruth described David putting on Saul's armor. Ruth said, "David resisted the urge to lead like someone else." Applying this idea to motherhood, have you been successful in walking in your own armor and leading like *you* should, or do you feel like you are still trying to walk in your mother's, mother-in-law's, or some other mother's footsteps?

How can we stay encouraged to keep walking in our own armor, even when we don't have an immediate victory like David?

Individual Activity: What Is God Saying to Me? (3 minutes)

Complete this activity on your own.

We just talked about wearing our own armor in leading as a mom. How can we ensure that we choose the right armor to begin with?

List the names of your children below. Next to each child's name, brainstorm one or more ways that you will connect that child's strength to God's story.

Closing Prayer (2 minutes)

Have one person close the session in prayer. Remember to pray for patience and wisdom as each mom sees her children transformed into God's image. Pray also for diligence in completing the between-sessions study. Enjoy your week, sisters!

Between-Sessions Personal Study

Scripture Memory Verse of the Week

Here is this week's gem. Be sure to keep this nugget of truth at the forefront of your mind and on the tip of your tongue.

> God works in different ways, but it is the same God who does the work in all of us.
>
> 1 Corinthians 12:6 NLT

Read and Learn

Read chapters nine and ten of the *Hoodwinked* book. Notes any questions you might have and copy down any phrases that give you inspiration.

It takes a parent, guided by God, and a little help from whomever he sends your child's way.

Just be prayerful.

And careful.

And willing to trust him to draw their hearts to his, even if in the drawing, a little detour is needed along the way. Remember, more is caught than is taught. And just *telling* children what is right and wrong, along with all the appropriate biblical backup available, doesn't always work.

(cont.)

Sometimes they have to learn lessons the old-fashioned and painfully hard way. Or perhaps at least learn them from someone other than you.

Is it time for you to call in some backup?

HOODWINKED, PAGES 131–132

Study and Reflect

1. In chapter nine of *Hoodwinked,* Karen said "the pathway of motherhood is paved with many stepping stones" (page 122). Before we became moms we may have envisioned a yellow brick road or a wide expressway to facilitate a speedy and glorious path to motherhood success. Then reality settled in, and our yellow bricks were more like little stones. Our fast paces were more like a baby crawling. How are you dealing with your current pathway of motherhood? Do you feel life is going faster or slower than expected? Or is it clipping along at the pace you thought it would?

   Briefly describe your current season of motherhood in the first stepping stone on the following page. In the second stone, write a description of the next step God is asking you to take for your family. If you don't know what the next step is, write a prayer to God asking him to reveal to you your next step.

   Now, between these two stones, copy the words of 2 Corinthians 5:7. You can take some time to get a little artsy (crayons, markers, colored pencils), or just write the verse in bold lettering. Let it be a visual reminder that the big and little steps through motherhood are done in faith.

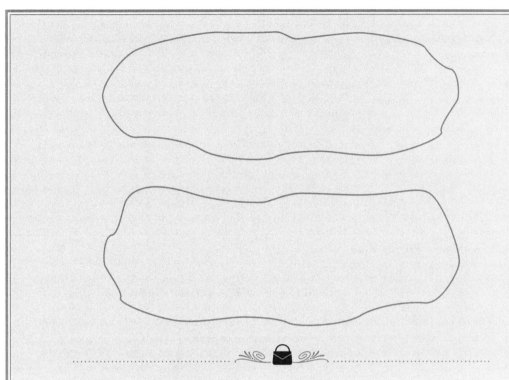

Jesus offers us living water—eternal life through faith in his finished work on the cross. Only through placing our trust in him can we have this life—life to the full. Christ promises to never leave or forsake us. He is with us for the long haul in this calling of motherhood if we will only trust in, rely on, and place our hope in him. With him we don't need to fear the future—neither our own future, nor that of our kids.

HOODWINKED, PAGES 128–129

2. Also in chapter nine (page 124), Karen quoted Bible teacher Warren Wiersbe: "God's *I am* is perfectly adequate for man's *I am not*." When have you felt yourself saying in defeat, "I am not . . ."? What were you going through at the time and why were you feeling overwhelmed?

Did you turn to God for strength? If so, how did he show you that his *I am* was greater?

3. In chapter nine Karen teaches us three key principles from the story of the biblical mother Hagar. They are listed here for you:

    ❀ 1. *God sees our situation.*
    ❀ 2. *God knows the needs of our children.*
    ❀ 3. *God will continue to provide living water for us in the days ahead.*

    Let's find one additional biblical example to reinforce each of these principles.

    Please read John 1:47–50. In the space below, explain how this supports the first principle: *God sees our situation.*

    Next, read Judges 13:2–5 and explain how this supports the second principle: *God knows the needs of our children.*

Finally, read Exodus 17:5–6 and explain how this supports the third principle: *God will continue to provide living water for us in the days ahead.*

4. Much of our conversation and study during this session has focused on walking in our own armor. During the video session and in chapter ten of *Hoodwinked*, Ruth encouraged us to use what works for us as we lead. Let's look at three biblical leaders who administered three very unconventional methods of warfare.

   Read 2 Chronicles 20:20–24. Fill in the following information:

   Leader's name:

   Did he experience victory or defeat?

   Unconventional details of the battle:

   Read Joshua 6:15–21. Fill in the following information:

   Leader's name:

Did he experience victory or defeat?

Unconventional details of the battle:

Read Judges 7:19–22. Fill in the following information:

Leader's name:

Did he experience victory or defeat?

Unconventional details of the battle:

5. Use the space below to write down this week's memory verse. (You'll find it at both the beginning and end of this personal study.)

How do Jehoshaphat, Joshua, and Gideon (from the portions of Scripture above) exemplify and aid us in understanding this session's memory verse?

Take a moment to ponder this statement from the *Hoodwinked* book.

> Uniqueness isn't just about who they [our children] will become, but who they are right now.
>
> HOODWINKED, PAGE 142

Hey, this quote is for you too! God is continuing to grow you into a unique, awesome mom. Though God might use some conventional methods and some unconventional ones, take heart, *it's the same God who works in all of us!* He has given us different jobs to do for him, so keep on walking in your own armor! As our memory verse for this session says:

> God works in different ways, but it is the same God who does the work in all of us.
>
> 1 CORINTHIANS 12:6 NLT

SESSION 6

Raising Children on Your Knees:

When Your Child Makes a Bad Choice

For it is written: As I live, says the Lord,
every knee will bow to Me, and every tongue
will give praise to God. So then, each of us
will give an account of himself to God.

ROMANS 14:11–12 (HCSB)

Checking In (10 minutes)

Welcome to the final session of *Hoodwinked*. We are nearing the end of our myth-busting and nearing the beginning of our new truth-living motherhood! Please share what you have learned. You know the routine by now; it doesn't matter if you haven't completed all the homework. It is more valuable to your sisters in Christ if you contribute to the conversation about what God is doing in your life. Each member's insights are important to have a full and rich group session experience!

- ❀ What from the session five video segment (about walking in your own armor) most challenged or encouraged you since we last met?
- ❀ Did you see any changes in your attitude toward parenting since last week?
- ❀ What truth from the last between-sessions study seemed to refresh or relieve you?

Video: Raising Children on Your Knees: When Your Child Makes a Bad Choice (22 minutes)

Play the video segment for session six. As you watch, record any thoughts or concepts that stand out to you in the outline that follows.

Notes

There's a misconception out there that our child's bad choice makes us a bad mom.

Do not tether your child's choice to the core of your identity.

Job 1:1–8

- ✿ Job got up and offered sacrifices on behalf of his children.
- ✿ He had a desire for his kids to walk in a manner worthy of the Lord.
- ✿ Although Job's kids were rabble-rousers, he was not.
- ✿ God said that Job was blameless.

Impeccable parents sometimes equal iffy kids.

What can we remember as we try to keep perspective in parenting through tough times?

You are your child's best teacher.

- ✿ Keep showing up for class.
- ✿ Keep teaching the lessons.
- ✿ Keep living the lessons.
- ✿ More is caught than taught.

When your child does make a bad choice, remember that everything good in your child is still there.

- ✿ Sometimes our child's bad decision is the result of a good quality.
- ✿ When our children are younger, it is because these qualities haven't matured yet.
- ✿ We are seeing the beginning of their testimony.

Do not tether the stellar or stupid choices of your child to your identity.

- ❀ If we can take credit for every bad choice in their life, then we could also take credit for every good choice in their life.
- ❀ Anything good and godly in our kids is because of God's grace and despite our parenting. Any bad choices they make, they own.
- ❀ Your kids will stop sinning the day that you do.

Raise your children on your knees.

- ❀ Prayer is active.
- ❀ Go to God in times of crisis and in the good times.
- ❀ Sometimes we need to stop talking to our kids about God and start talking to God about our kids.

When your friend's child makes a bad choice, don't throw stones. Bake her banana bread.

Never say never in motherhood. One day you might need some banana bread yourself and a shoulder to cry on.

Parenting is not a recipe; parenting is a relationship—with both God and our children.

In our relationship with the Lord, our kids need to see the potential for their relationship with the Lord.

Let's run to God when we fail *and* when we get it right.

Let's not let the world leave us hoodwinked. Let's allow the Lord to make us holy as, through the ups and downs of motherhood, we become more like his Son.

Group Discussion (10 minutes)

Take a few minutes to discuss what you just watched.

1. What part of Karen's teaching had the greatest impact on you?

2. Karen mentioned that she used to believe little equations about mothering, such as "crying baby = bad mom." Did you have any preconceived equations about motherhood before you had children? What were they?

3. Did you find that having these equations/expectations was helpful or hurtful to your motherhood and why?

4. Karen shared Job 1:1–8 during the video. Have a group member reread these verses aloud. What did you take away from Karen's thoughts on this passage?

Cluster Group Discussion (8 minutes)

If your group is comprised of more than twelve members, consider completing this discussion in smaller groups of three to six people each.

5. Read Matthew 8:23–27 together. What do you think the disciples learned here that was more "caught than taught"?

Did Jesus specifically say why he allowed this event to happen? Do you think this situation encouraged the disciples to "think on their own"?

Karen said that we are our child's best teacher. How do you think Jesus was the best teacher to his disciples in this passage?

Did Jesus take ownership for the disciples' lack of faith? Or was their faith … well, *their* faith?

What does that last answer tell us about teaching and motherhood?

Group Discussion (15 minutes)

Gather back together as one large group and answer the following questions.

6. Have each group share some of their answers to the cluster group discussion.

7. Let's look at another passage that highlights the relationship between Jesus and the disciples. Have a volunteer read Mark 14:27–31, 66–72.

   The first observation worth making is that Jesus knew what was going to happen before it happened. Sometimes we moms see things coming a mile away and sometimes we are blindsided by something our child does. How did Jesus know that Peter was going to deny him? Think of as many reasons as possible.

   Which reasons can we aspire to have in our relationship with our kids?

   In the video, Karen taught that when our child makes a bad choice, we need to remember that everything good in our child is still there. Consider verses 66–72 again. Do you believe that Peter remembered Jesus' prediction as he denied even knowing Jesus? Really think about and then discuss what could have been happening spiritually, mentally, and physically to Peter as he was being questioned.

   Of all the things you just noted as possibly happening to Peter, I'm guessing no one suggested that his identity had been erased. Peter was still Peter. Peter was just Peter going through a hard time. A test. A test he didn't do very well on.

8. Now, have a volunteer read John 21:15–19. How did Jesus treat Peter in this post-resurrection appearance?

Even after Peter betrayed Jesus, the Lord still trusted him enough to give him new responsibility: "Feed my sheep." How does this make a hard case against using the phrase "I told you so" with our kids when they mess up? How does it speak to you about giving your children another chance to earn your trust?

Did Jesus tether Peter's prior decision in Mark 14 to his identity in John 21? How does this challenge you as a mom?

Individual Activity: What Is God Saying to Me? (3 minutes)

Complete this activity on your own.

Take a prayerful minute or two to ponder some decisions that your child (or one of your children) has made. Have you wrongly tethered your identity to your child's bad choice? Has this session helped you transport your thoughts to a better place? Take the space below to write a statement that counteracts the lie that your child's bad choice means you are a bad mom.

Closing Prayer (2 minutes)

Today we discussed some heavy aspects of parenting. In the video, Karen said, "Our kids will stop sinning when we stop sinning." Take some time to pray together that God will be glorified as we moms seek not to be perfect parents but prayerful parents. Pray that we will "keep showing up for class" and will tether our identity only to Christ.

Final Personal Study

Scripture Memory Verse of the Week

Here is our last memory verse for the *Hoodwinked* study. Memorize not only the words of this passage but also its meaning. It will prove to be a strong truth to hold onto when we are tempted to worry that we will have to give an account for the mistakes of our children.

> For it is written: As I live, says the Lord, every knee will bow to Me, and every tongue will give praise to God. So then, each of us will give an account of himself to God.
>
> ROMANS 14:11–12 HCSB

Read and Learn

Read chapters eleven and twelve in the *Hoodwinked* book. Jot down any notes or highlight any sections of the reading that are relevant to your current situation.

Study and Reflect

1. During the previous between-sessions study, we very briefly looked at some verses relating to Samson and the instructions that his parents received before his birth. Let's look at what happened next in this story. Read Judges 13:24–14:9.

In the space below, write down the key phrase of Judges 13:25.

At the beginning of Judges 14, what decision was Samson making and how do we know that it didn't thrill his parents?

In the space below, write down the key phrase (first phrase) of Judges 14:4.

Look back at the two key phrases you wrote down. What insights does this give us into things that happen with our children that we did not want to happen? Could something else be going on? If so, what?

Reread Judges 14:9. It was not a big deal to eat honey, but it was a huge deal to touch a dead animal at that time. By returning to the dead carcass and retrieving the honey within, Samson committed a sin. His parents would have been sinning also *if* they had known where it came from. What does the end of verse 9 say?

Had Samson's parents known that he killed the lion or that they were eating defiled honey, do you think they would have acted differently?

2. Consider Myth #10: My Child's Bad Choice Means I'm a Bad Mom. The mom who says this doesn't take into consideration whether she knows all the facts of the situation. We cannot be responsible for what we don't know. *However*, how might this small story of Samson have been different if his parents had asked more questions? Name a few specific details that likely would have gone differently.

    Briefly explain why ignorance is not bliss—especially in motherhood.

    Contrast any details of Peter and Jesus' relationship (questions 7 and 8 of the group discussion) to Samson and his parents.

3. In the video, Karen mentioned that it has been said that God is the perfect parent and yet his first two children, Adam and Eve, committed the first sin. God did not take responsibility for this. Who was held responsible for their decision? (Refresh your memory by reading Genesis 3:8–21.)

What were the consequences of Adam and Eve's sin?

What is significant about the end of verse 21?

God asked questions in verses 8–13. God gave consequences for their sin in verses 14–19. God clothed them in verse 21. God did a lot, but he did not change his identity because of what Adam and Eve chose to do. Why do we as moms feel our identity is changed—or even tarnished—because of the bad decisions of our kids?

Going a little deeper, have you ever gotten angry with God because of something foolish your child did? Is God any less good when we face a motherhood crisis? Are we any less of a mom when we face a motherhood crisis? Record your thoughts below.

It is in our total reliance on him for our lifestyles and answers that we forge a deep faith, one that finds us throwing ourselves on Jesus, saturating ourselves with God's Word, and raising our kids on our knees as deep in prayer as we are in laundry and homework and life.

So run to him, mom. Run away from the myths. Jump with abandon into the arms of the Truth himself. The Way. The Truth. And the Life. Like a loving father who has gained his toddler's complete trust. Run. Jump. Land and be held.

The ride is sometimes scary. The twists and turns play games with our insides until we aren't quite sure how much more we can stomach. But he is faithful. Always faithful. He will never leave you to walk alone but will carry you each step of the way, if only you will let him.

We believe in you, mom. Be hoodwinked no more. Let the truth of these words sink into your soul.

And then . . . love lavishly and mother well.

HOODWINKED, PAGE 193

4. As a review activity, write down the ten myths of motherhood in the space provided on the next two pages. After each myth, write down one phrase or statement that stands out from the book, study guide, Bible, or video teaching that will really help you remember why it's not true.

1. _____

2. _____

3. _____

4. _____

5. _____

6. _____

7. _____

8. _____

9. _____

10. _____

5. Which motherhood myth(s) did you believe before doing this study? Has your thinking on any of them changed after completing the study? How do you feel your parenting will change without this deception lingering in your life?

Which biblical illustration challenged your current parenting most and why? Take a minute to glance back over your notes in this study guide.

Finish this sentence with your own words:

I DON'T WANT TO BE THE PERFECT MOM, I JUST WANT TO BE . . .

Hoodwinked No More

Moms who are no longer hoodwinked are moms who are free. The Bible says "Then you will know the truth, and the truth will set you free" (John 8:32). We are free to feed our kids Goldfish crackers or organic apple slices. We are free to send our child to public school or to homeschool. We are free to potty-train early or late. We are free.

There are some moms who ask questions out of *curiosity*, there are some moms who ask questions to *compare*, and there are some moms who ask questions because they are scared out of their mind and need a little *courage*. You can't always know what kind of mom you are talking to, but like Jesus, if you take some time, you will see her heart. When you do, engage her in some myth-busting. Think of how you would want to be treated. Remember to say everything with "gentleness and respect." Remember to bring some banana bread. Remember that the only thing better than raising your kids on your knees is to have another mom beside you.

Prayer of Commitment

Close out this personal study by spending a few moments in prayer. Ask God to continue to guide you as you seek to be a mom after his own heart—a follower who is learning, step-by-step, to stop believing the myths of motherhood and live the truth instead. Make this prayer time one of commitment to living life according to his plan for you.

Final Note from the Authors

Oh how we wish we were together face-to-face! As you finished your last day of this study, we would give you a hug and celebrate with some banana bread and coffee. Please allow us to share our hopes with you.

We hope you have allowed the Lord to love and teach you over the past few weeks, deepening your relationship with him.

We hope you will apply the biblical principles pointed out on these pages—the very ones that can help you to feel empowered and not empty.

We hope you feel equipped to be the unique mom God had in mind when he made your children yours—whether they grew in your womb or in your heart through adoption.

We hope that you will continue to commit God's Word to memory, thereby saving you worry and giving you perspective.

And we hope that long after this book has been placed on a shelf, passed on to a friend, or donated to charity, that you'll still be reading The Book daily—God's go-to instruction manual for life.

Time for us to use our words one last time. This time as we have the privilege of praying for you.

> *Father, we lift the mother reading these words up to you right now. You know her anxious thoughts. You see her greatest fears. You hear her deepest cries in the night. We trust you, dear Lord, and know that you always know what is best for us and for our kids. You do not make mistakes. There is nothing that takes you by surprise. Each child. Each situation. Each joy and each sorrow are all allowed in our lives on purpose. May they not make us fretful. May they not make us bitter. May they not cause us to give up but to walk ever closer with you. We want to believe the truth. And live the truth. Because you, O Lord, are the Truth that frees us. The Way that steers us. And the very Life—exceedingly abundant and gloriously everlasting. Into your care we place our fears and commit our children's future. We love you, Father. Please perfectly parent us as we mother, freed from all the myths and tethered to the Truth. In Jesus' name. Amen.*

Karen & Ruth

BONUS
ACTIVITIES

Ideas for a Bonus Session Seven or
Bridge Building with Other Moms

Now that the six video sessions have come to a close, your group might like to meet one more time to discuss the material you read in chapters eleven and twelve of *Hoodwinked*.

Following are some ideas and suggestions not only for a bonus seventh session but also for a possible bridge building get-together between you and another mom (or two). Also included are some yummy recipes to make your bonus session part study – part party or to gift to another mom as you reach out to her.

BONUS
SESSION 7

No More
Hoodwinked Moms

Opener (5 minutes)

Okay. Memory test time. See how many of the myths of motherhood you can recall as a group. Have everyone shut her copy of the *Hoodwinked* book except for one person. Have that person turn to the table of contents where all ten myths are listed and check off each one your group mentions. Ready? Get set. GO!

Group Discussion (20 minutes)

1. Since the group was last together, we read chapters eleven and twelve of *Hoodwinked*. Take a few moments to glance back over these chapters and then share any thoughts with the group.

    Was there anything you highlighted, were struck by, or had a question about in chapter eleven?

    Was there anything you highlighted, were struck by, or had a question about in chapter twelve?

    How about from last session's video segment?

2. In chapter eleven of *Hoodwinked*, Karen tells of a time her son made a bad choice. Yet from that experience she discovered some of his good character qualities: he

is compassionate; he roots for the downtrodden; he is a good entrepreneur; etc. Without going into too much detail or betraying any confidences, can you share about a time when your child (or yourself as a child, teen, or young adult) made a bad choice that nevertheless displayed good character qualities?

3. If you wish to share, tell of one aspect of motherhood that has surprised you most. Is it how often you have to do laundry? How much money groceries cost for a household that includes teenage boys? How little time alone you get with your husband for "horizontal fellowship" (if you are tracking with me, ladies!)? Or, is it something more serious—like how much your heart is crushed when a child goes off to college or makes a bad decision?

Individual Activity: What Is God Saying to Me? (5 minutes)

Complete this activity on your own.

As you take a few minutes alone, ask God to bring to mind which of the ten myths you most believed or struggle not to believe still. Then write a short prayer to God about this myth and your thoughts and feelings about it.

Group Discussion (20 minutes)

Gather as one large group again for the following questions.

4. Look back over the study guide questions you answered during the personal study time after session six. If you would like to share any of your answers to question 5 (see pages 110–111), please do so. The individual questions are printed again here for easy reference.

   ❀ Which motherhood myth(s) did you believe before doing this study? Has your thinking on any of them changed after completing the study? How do you feel your parenting will change without this deception lingering in your life?
   ❀ Which biblical illustration challenged your current parenting most and why? Take a minute to glance back over your notes in this study guide.
   ❀ Finish this sentence with your own words: I DON'T WANT TO BE THE PERFECT MOM, I JUST WANT TO BE . . .

Search the Scriptures

5. Briefly look back over your notes in the study guide, anything you highlighted in the *Hoodwinked* book (including the Ten Memory Verses for the Too-Busy Mom on pages 209–212), or the weekly memory verses found in this study guide on page 133. As you feel led, share one or two verses or passages of Scripture that you learned the most from during this study and why.

One Last Look at *Hoodwinked*

6. If you could pick just one concept, idea, story, or encouragement from the book *Hoodwinked*, what might you most likely be able to recall a year from now because of its lasting impact?

Closing Prayer (3 minutes)

Have one member close the group in prayer. Or, if you wish, you may have the women break into small groups of two to four for prayer time.

Let's Eat!

If your group is having refreshments, let the party begin! Recipe ideas are provided, starting on page 123.

Ideas for Mom Bridge Building

We moms are busy, but most of us desire deeper connections with other moms. Here are some ways you can reach out to other mothers—both those with whom you are already friends and those you either don't know as well or who mother differently than you. Try out one of the suggested activities or actions that follow. And don't forget to give her a food gift—either one of the recipes included in this study guide or one of your own. Now, get out there and build that bridge!

❀ If you are a mom who works full-time outside of the home, invite a stay-at-home mom to go out to lunch or coffee with you. Be intentional to ask about the lives of her children and about her current prayer requests as a mother. If, on the flipside, you are a mom who is at home full-time, do the same with a mom who is employed outside the home.

❀ Is there a mother you know whose children are educated differently than yours? Make a point to show interest in her children's education. For example, if your children are homeschooled but another mother's children attend public school, go on the school's website to check out its activity schedule. Are they hosting a fundraiser or putting on a Christmas concert? Take your children to one of these events. Invite the other mother and her children to join you and yours for a treat at a local eatery after the activity is finished. Or, if you are the one with children in public school, take an interest in your friend who educates her children at home. Homeschooled children also have activities such as sports or science fairs. Ask the other mother if one of these activities is coming up. Then, take along your children to watch her kids play or participate. You can go out for a bite to eat when the event is over.

❀ Do you know another mother who is having a hard time due to the choices of one of her children? Make one of the suggested treats for her and show up at her house unannounced to deliver it. Offer to pray with her if she has time for you to visit for a moment. Remember—don't throw stones. Bake banana bread!

❀ Host a Mug and Muffin night. Invite a variety of moms you know over for an evening visit. Make sure they don't all live similar lives. (Include those of different ages and mothering stages and philosophies.) Ask a few of the moms to bring various types of muffins (see pages 123–124 for recipe options) and a mug. You provide hot drinks—coffee, teas, flavored cocoas—and plates and napkins for the muffins. You can have an informal time just visiting or do something more formal, such as watching a video together or sharing prayer requests and then praying. Or, you can have an idea sharing night where everyone brings their favorite DIY idea to share or you hold a recipe swap where everyone brings enough copies of their favorite family-pleasing main dish, side dish, and dessert so you all can get some new menu ideas.

❀ Is there a mom you know who is struggling? Is she overwhelmed with small children at home and has little time to herself? Or maybe she is stressed from raising teenagers. Arrange for her to be granted an official Mom's Day Off. Inform her that on the day of her choosing, you—and possibly your children if they are old enough—will be treating her children to a fun day in your care while she treats herself to a day off from mothering responsibilities. Give her a basket with some goodies just for her—some fancy chocolate, a fun coffee mug, a scarf or fluffy-comfy socks, a new book, a gift card to a local coffee house or restaurant, or a gift certificate for a spa or nail service or to take in a movie all by herself. She will be thrilled with the time alone! Be sure to attach a gift tag to her Mom's Day Off basket (see page 127). The tag has a space for you to leave your contact information so she can call to arrange for her day off.

~~RECIPES:~~
Muffins and Cupcakes
and Breads, Oh My!

For centuries people have bonded over food. As we break bread (or share a cinnamon cappuccino muffin—yum!), we also share our hearts.

Use these tasty recipes as you host a seventh bonus session. Or whip up a batch of treats with your kids tonight and then go brighten someone's day. You'll be helping—even if in just a little way—to build a bridge with another mom. Don't forget to include one of the whimsical tags (provided right after the recipes) with your baked good. Just photocopy the tag of your choice on colored card stock, cut it out, punch a hole in it with a hole-punch, and attach it to your goodies with some curly ribbon. Adorable!

ᴥ Cinnamon Cappuccino Muffins ᴥ

These moist muffins win rave reviews every time in our circle of mom friends. Perfect with a steaming cup of coffee! You may make them with cinnamon chips or semisweet chocolate chips.

Ingredients:

Espresso Frosting
6 oz. cream cheese, softened
3 T. butter, softened
¾ – 1 c. powdered sugar (or more)
½ t. instant coffee granules
¼ t. almond extract
¼ c. miniature semisweet chocolate chips

Muffins
2 c. all-purpose flour
¾ c. sugar

2½ t. baking powder
1 t. cinnamon
⅛ t. nutmeg
½ t. salt
1 c. whole milk
2 T. instant coffee granules
½ c. butter, melted
1 egg, beaten
1 t. vanilla extract
¾ c. cinnamon (or semisweet chocolate) chips

For the frosting: In a bowl, combine all frosting ingredients except chocolate chips and beat with an electric mixer until smooth. Adjust amount of sugar as needed until frosting is a spreadable consistency. Stir in chocolate chips and set aside.

For muffins: In a large bowl, combine flour, sugar, baking powder, cinnamon, nutmeg, and salt. In another bowl, combine milk and coffee granules, stirring until coffee is completely dissolved. Add melted butter, egg, and vanilla. Mix well. Stir into dry ingredients just until combined and then fold in cinnamon (or semisweet chocolate) chips.

Fill paper-lined muffin cups two-thirds full. Bake at 375 degrees for 18–20 minutes or until a toothpick inserted near the center comes out clean. Cool for 5 minutes before removing from pans to wire racks. Cool and frost. Makes 12–14 muffins.

‿ Mango-Macadamia Muffins ‿

Try your hand at these mouth-watering and oh-so-different muffins that Karen's sister-in-love was famous for making at her Florida bed-and-breakfast, The Mango Inn, back when she still owned it. They are a unique treat that is sure to perk up anyone's day!

Ingredients:

1 large egg
½ c. sour cream
½ c. milk
1 t. vanilla
4 T. butter, melted and cooled
½ c. diced ripe mango
2 c. flour
½ c. sugar
1 T. baking powder

¼ t. baking soda
¼ t. salt

Topping:
⅓ c. chopped unsalted macadamia nuts
¼ c. flour
¼ c. light brown sugar
¼ t. cinnamon
2 T. softened butter

For topping: Combine all topping ingredients in a small bowl. Mash until combined. Chill until needed.

Preheat oven to 400 degrees. In a large bowl whisk together egg, sour cream, milk, vanilla, and melted butter. Fold in mango.

In another bowl, stir together dry ingredients. Add wet ingredients. Fold together just to moisten. Batter will be lumpy.

Quickly fill greased muffin tins with batter to the tops. Crumble topping over the tops.

Bake 25–30 minutes until a toothpick inserted comes out with just a few crumbs clinging to it. Cool 5–10 minutes. Remove carefully from pans.

Serve warm or at room temperature. Makes 12 muffins.

≈≈ Better-Than-Bakery Cupcakes ≈≈

Okay. Seriously. You will not believe these shortcut cupcakes aren't from scratch. This doctored-up mix recipe is so easy and scrumptious! (Shhh!! Your secret is safe with us!)

Ingredients:
½ c. butter—NOT margarine, melted
1 box cake mix—whatever flavor you choose! (a mix with pudding works best)
1 c. (minus 1 t.) water (measure water in a cup, then take out one teaspoon)
3 large eggs, slightly beaten

In a small saucepan, melt the butter over very low heat. (You can melt it in the microwave but be very careful not to overdo or burn!) Cool slightly. In a large bowl, mix butter and cake mix. Add water and eggs and mix on low speed with an electric mixer just until incorporated. Then, mix on high for 1 minute. Place in 22–24 paper liners in a muffin tin. Bake at 350 degrees for 18–20 minutes. Watch carefully and do not overbake. Remove. Cool. Frost with your favorite frosting. Add sprinkles. Or coconut. Or mini-chocolate chips. Or colored sugar. Go wild and crown yourself the Cupcake Queen! Everyone will think you slaved all day making these babies from scratch.

↬ Chocolate Chip Banana Bread ↫

Remember in session six when Karen encouraged us not to throw stones at other moms but to bake banana bread instead? Here is her go-to recipe.

Ingredients:

1¾ c. all-purpose flour
¾ c. granulated sugar
1 t. baking powder
½ t. baking soda
½ t. salt
1 t. ground cinnamon
1 c. mashed, very ripe bananas (about 3 bananas)

1¼ t. pure vanilla extract (not imitation)
2 eggs, lightly beaten
½ c. butter (not margarine)
1 c. semisweet chocolate chips (you may also use peanut butter chips or coarsely chopped walnuts or pecans)

Preheat the oven to 375 degrees. Grease and flour a 9" x 5" x 3" loaf pan. You may also use a cooking spray that is made specifically for baking that has flour in it. In a large bowl, combine all dry ingredients, mixing well. In a small saucepan, melt the butter thoroughly and then cool slightly (don't allow it to solidify). Using a mixer on low speed, in a second medium-sized bowl, slowly mix the vanilla and eggs until they are well incorporated. Add in the mashed banana and mix until well combined. Then slowly drizzle in the melted, cooled butter until it is combined thoroughly. (Make sure the butter is not still hot or it will cook the raw eggs!) Then, gently add the banana mixture to the dry ingredients and stir just until they are fully combined. Be very careful not to overmix or the bread will not be moist. Finally, by hand, lightly stir in the chocolate chips. Spoon into the prepared loaf pan and level out well. Bake for 45–55 minutes, watching carefully to not overbake. Test with a cake tester or toothpick to make sure the bread is cooked all the way through. Remove and cool 15 minutes before turning onto a cooling rack. Allow bread to cool to room temperature. Wrap tightly in foil and let sit one day at room temperature before eating.

*I thank my God every time
I remember you.*

PHILIPPIANS 1:3

*You are a great mom
and I believe in you!*

*Taste and see that the LORD
is good; blessed is the one who
takes refuge in him.*

 PSALM 34:8

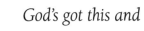

*Relax, Mom.
God's got this and
I am praying for you!*

NOTICE: Please Claim Your Prize — A Mom's Day Off!!

Congratulations! Due to your hard work and stellar performance in your often-thankless job of being a mother, you have been awarded a Mom's Day Off! On the day of your choice, your kids will be well cared for and given a day of fun while you take some time to yourself! Go out and shop or stay home and sleep. The day is all yours to do whatever you'd like! To claim your prize and choose your day off, contact _____ by calling _____.

❀ *Congrats, Mom! You deserve it!* ❀

Minute-Long Mom Pep Talks
from *Hoodwinked*

Following are some brief quotes from the *Hoodwinked* book designed for you to photocopy and place where you will see them often. We pray these little pep talks will help you to find and maintain your perspective as you mother your children.

We moms are never going to be perfect. Not our homes. Not our method of discipline. Not our food. Not our schedule. When we keep these mythical mosaics of perfection as our goal, we only set ourselves up for sure failure. We need to stop pursuing the appearance of perfection. (Yes, the *appearance* of perfection. There is no such thing as actual perfection.) We must start instead to pursue the person Jesus Christ.

God has set apart the home as his. Home is a place where his presence is to be felt and his purposes are to be pursued. He places parents in those homes as watchmen, pastors, priests, shepherds, teachers, and warriors who have been called and commissioned to pass on their faith to their children for the sake of the world.

Of course, take pleasure being a mom. It will bring you delight often. However, true joy comes from serving Jesus. If you hang your hat of happiness on being a mom, you will experience despair during the down times or when your child isn't making good and godly choices. Get your true joy from being a follower of Jesus, not from being the mom of so-and-so.

The importance of what we do for God is not contingent upon how many *people* see what we do. God measures our faithfulness to him (and our families) the same, whether others see it or not. Is the "divine nod" of the God who sees enough for you?

Rules may change behavior, but they cannot change the heart. Our children need our love and not just our law.

If we want our children to be disciples of Jesus, then we must first be parents who are disciples of Jesus. You will pass on what you possess.

We should number our days not so we live fearfully, but in an effort to live more faithfully. Our time as a mom is not infinite or limitless. We count our days so we can make them count.

Do not tether your identity to the choices of your child, whether stellar or stupid. We are not our child's choices. Their choices and their behavior are their own.

Parenting is not a recipe. Parenting is a relationship. A relationship with Christ and with our children. As we grow in our vertical relationship with the Lord, we will also grow in our relationship with our children. Yes, we will make mistakes. Yes, we will regret what we say or do sometimes. However, if our children see us continually going back to Christ when we blow it or giving him credit when we do make a wise choice, they too may want to have a relationship with him, one that is alive and active and growing. So let's tear up those recipe cards. Toss the maternal cookbooks. Log off the "how to raise perfect kids" websites. Run to Jesus. Both when you fail and when you get it right.

Scripture Memory Verses

For your convenience, the memory verses for this study are printed here in the size of a standard business card. Feel free to photocopy this page on card stock and then cut out the verses. You can then purchase a portable business card holder to keep them in and carry them with you throughout your day. This way, you can memorize and practice reciting your verses in the car pool line, waiting room, on lunch hour—any time you have a few spare minutes. Be sure to check to see if any members of your group want to arrive early to the sessions to practice reciting the verses from memory for each other.

SESSION 1

Be completely humble and gentle; be patient, bearing with one another in love. Make every effort to keep the unity of the Spirit through the bond of peace.

(EPHESIANS 4:2–3)

SESSION 2

Let us not become weary in doing good, for at the proper time we will reap a harvest if we do not give up.

(GALATIANS 6:9)

SESSION 3

Be very careful, then, how you live—not as unwise but as wise, making the most of every opportunity, because the days are evil. Therefore do not be foolish, but understand what the Lord's will is.

(EPHESIANS 5:15–17)

SESSION 4

"Come to me, all you who are weary and burdened, and I will give you rest. Take my yoke upon you and learn from me, for I am gentle and humble in heart, and you will find rest for your souls. For my yoke is easy and my burden is light."

(MATTHEW 11:28–30)

SESSION 5

God works in different ways, but it is the same God who does the work in all of us.

(1 CORINTHIANS 12:6 NLT)

SESSION 6

For it is written: As I live, says the Lord, every knee will bow to Me, and every tongue will give praise to God. So then, each of us will give an account of himself to God.

(ROMANS 14:11–12 HCSB)

About the Authors

Karen Ehman is a Proverbs 31 Ministries speaker, a *New York Times* bestselling author, and a writer for *Encouragement for Today*, an online devotional that reaches over one million women daily. She has written eight books including *Keep It Shut: What to Say, How to Say It & When to Say Nothing at All*. Married to her college sweetheart, Todd, and the mother of three, she enjoys antique hunting, cheering for the Detroit Tigers baseball team, and feeding the many teens who gather around her kitchen island for a taste of Mama Karen's cooking. Connect with her at www.karenehman.com.

Ruth Schwenk is the creator of The Better Mom website (www. thebettermom.com), and, along with her husband, the creator of For the Family (www.forthefamily.org), a site designed to equip and encourage parents. She is a pastor's wife, mom of four energetic kids, a lover of good coffee, and a dreamer of big dreams. She loves leading, speaking, blogging, and encouraging her audience to better themselves as they grow to be more like Christ. A graduate of Moody Bible Institute, Ruth has been serving with her husband full-time in local church ministry for over fifteen years.

Proverbs 31
MINISTRIES

ABOUT PROVERBS 31 MINISTRIES

Karen Ehman is an author, speaker, and online devotion writer for Proverbs 31 Ministries, located in Charlotte, North Carolina.

If you were inspired by *Hoodwinked* and desire to deepen your own personal relationship with Jesus Christ, we encourage you to connect with Proverbs 31 Ministries.

We exist to be a trusted friend who will take you by the hand and walk by your side, leading you one step closer to the heart of God through:

- Free online daily devotions
- Online Bible studies
- Daily radio programs
- Books and resources

For more information about Proverbs 31 Ministries, visit: www.Proverbs31.org.

To inquire about having Karen speak at your event, visit www.Proverbs31.org and click on "speakers."

Now that you have learned how to reject the lies and start walking in the truth in this journey of motherhood, wouldn't it be great to connect with other moms?

TheBetterMom.com is the place for you!

At The Better Mom our mission is to build God-honoring homes by inspiring moms to be better moms through sharing life and learning together.

We are moms who desire to be "better" even though we are busy. We believe God has placed a high calling on our lives as we:

- Raise children to impact the world
- Take care of our homes
- Love our husbands
- Ultimately honor God with our lives

We would love to have you join our community and share in our journey!

Join us today at

www.TheBetterMom.com

Hoodwinked

Ten Myths Moms Believe & Why We Need To Knock It Off

Karen Ehman and Ruth Schwenk

Moms have been hoodwinked—tricked into believing lies that keep them from not only enjoying motherhood but forging friendships with other moms who might tackle the tasks of motherhood differently. Myths such as "Mothering is natural, easy, and instinctive" cause moms to feel like failures if they have questions or apprehensions in raising their kids. Operating from the premise that "The way I mother is the right (and only) way" puts up fences between moms instead of building bridges of encouragement between them. Lies such as "I am my child's choices" tempt moms to mistakenly believe that if their child makes a wrong choice then they, in turn, must be a bad mom.

In their encouraging "we've been there" style, Karen Ehman and Ruth Schwenk enable mothers to:

- Identify ten myths of motherhood
- Replace the lies with the truth of what God says
- Acquire practical tools to help them form new and improved thought patterns and healthy behaviors
- Forge healthy, supportive relationships with other moms of all ages and stages
- Confidently embrace the calling of motherhood as they care for their families in their own unique way

Keep It Shut

What to Say, How to Say It, and When to Say Nothing at All

Karen Ehman

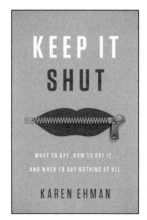

From Bible times to modern times, women have struggled with their words. What to say and how to say it. What not to say. When it is best to remain silent. And what to do when you've said something you wish you could now take back. In this book a woman whose mouth has gotten her into loads of trouble shares the hows (and how-not-tos) of dealing with the tongue.

Beyond just a "how not to gossip" book, this book explores what the Bible says about the many ways we are to use our words and the times when we are to remain silent. Karen will cover using our speech to interact with friends, coworkers, family, and strangers as well as in the many places we use our words in private, in public, online, and in prayer. Even the words we say silently to ourselves. She will address unsolicited opinion-slinging, speaking the truth in love, not saying words just to people-please, and dealing with our verbal anger.

Christian women struggle with their mouths. Even though we know that Scripture has much to say about how we are—and are not—to use our words, this is still an immense issue, causing heartache and strain not only in family relationships, but also in friendships, work, and church settings.

Six-session DVD study also available.

Available in stores and online!

Let. It. Go.

How to Stop Running the Show and Start Walking in Faith

Karen Ehman

Many women are wired to control. You're the ones who make sure the house is clean, the meals are prepared, the beds are made, the children are dressed, and everyone gets to work, school, and other activities on time.

But trying to control everything can be exhausting, and it can also cause friction with your friends and family.

This humorous, yet thought-provoking book guides you as you discover for yourself the freedom and reward of living a life "out of control," in which you allow God to be seated in the rightful place in your life. Armed with relevant biblical and current examples (both to emulate and to avoid), doable ideas, new thought patterns, and practical tools to implement, *Let. It. Go.* will gently lead you out of the land of over-control and into a place of quiet trust.

Six-session DVD study also available.